Journal of a First Fleet Surgeon (1788)

by

George B. Worgan
(1757-1838)

Surgeon of the Sirius

Note: The text follows Worgan's text as it was written. Sometimes he inserted phrases and extra information, and on one occasion returned to a blank page and inserted a description of the French ships at Botany Bay in the midst of his entry for 22 January.

Contents

Sirius, Sydney Cove, Port Jackson--June 12th 1788.

Dear Richard.

I think I hear You saying, "Where the D--ce is Sydney Cove Port Jackson"? and see You whirling the Letter about to find out the Name of the Scribe: Perhaps You have taken up Salmons Gazetteer, if so, pray spare your Labour, and attend to Me for half an Hour--We sailed from the Cape of Good Hope on the 12th of November 1787-- As that was the last civilized Country We should touch at, in our Passage to Botany Bay We provided ourselves with every Article, necessary for the forming a civilized Colony, Live Stock, consisting of Bulls, Cows, Horses Mares, Colts, Sheep, Hogs, Goats Fowls and other living Creatures by Pairs. We likewise, procured a vast Number of Plants, Seeds & other Garden articles, such, as Orange, Lime, Lemon, Quince Apple, Pear Trees, in a Word, every Vegetable Production that the Cape afforded. Thus Equipped, each Ship like another Noah's Ark, away we steered for Botany Bay, and after a tolerably pleasant Voyage of 10 Weeks & 2 Days Governor Phillip, had the Satisfaction to see the whole of his little Fleet safe at Anchor in the said Bay.

As we were sailing in We saw 8 or 10 of the Natives, sitting on the Rocks on the South Shore, and as the Ships bordered pretty near thereto, we could hear them hollow, and observe them talking to one another very earnestly, at the same time pointing towards the Ships; they were of a black reddish sooty Colour, entirely naked, walked very upright, and each of them had long Spears and a short Stick in their hands, soon after the Ships had anchored, the Indians went up into the Wood, lit a Fire, and sat Around about it, as unconcerned (apparently,) as tho' nothing had occurred to them. Two Boats from the Sirius, were now Manned and armed, and the Governor, accompanied by Cap.tn Hunter, and several other Officers, went towards the Shore, where they had seen the Natives, who perceiving the Boats making towards the Beach, came out of the Wood, and walked along, some distance from the Water-side, but immediately on the Boats landing, they scampered up into the Woods again, with great Precipitation. On this, the Governor, advised, that we should seem quite indifferent about them, and this apparent Indifference had a good Effect, for they very soon appeared in sight of Us, When, the Governor held up some Beads, Red Cloth & other Bawbles and made signs for them to advance, but they still were exceedingly shy & timid, and would not be enticed by our allurements; which the Governor perceiving, He shewed them his Musket, then laid it on the Ground, advancing singly towards them, they now seeing that He had nothing in his Hands like a Weapon one of ye oldest of the Natives gave his Spears to a younger, and approached to meet the Governor, but not without discovering manifest tokens of Fear, and distrust, making signs for the things to be laid on the Ground which, the Governor complying with, He advanced, tooke them up, and went back to his Companions; Another, came forth and wanted some of the same kind of Presents, which, were given to Him by the same Method, at length, after various Methods to impress them with the Belief that We meant them no harm, they suffered Us to come up to them, and after making them all presents, which they received with much the same kind of Pleasure, which Children shew at such Bawbles, just looking at them, then holding out their Hands for more, some laughing heartily, and jumping extravagantly; they began to shew a Confidence, and became very familiar, and curious about our Cloaths, feeling the Coat, Waistcoat, and even the Shirt and on seeing one of the Gentlemen(Unclear:), pull off his Hat, they all set up a loud Hoop, one was curious enough to take hold of a Gentlemans Hair that was cued, and called to his Companions to look at it, this was the occasion of another loud Hoop, accompanied with other Emotions of Astonishment. In a Word, they seemed pretty well divested of their Fears, and became very funny Fellows.

They suffered the Sailors to dress them with different coloured Papers, and Fools-Caps, which pleased them mightily, the strange contrast these Decorations made with their black Complexion brought strongly to my Mind, the Chimney-Sweepers in London on a May-Day.--They were all Men & Boys in this Tribe.

I should have told You, that the Governor, left the Sirius soon after we sailed from the Cape of Good Hope; and Embarked on Board the Supply Brig & Gave up the Command of ye Convoy to Cap.tn Hunter, in order that he might proceed on before the main Body of the Fleet, but he arrived in Botany Bay, only two Days before Us. In this Time, He had obtained an Intercourse or two, with some Natives on the North Shore, but, as the Means which he took to gain their Confidence, and effect a Parley, were much the same as those, I have given you an account of, I shall only mention a few singular Circumstances that occurred in these Intercourses. The Supply Brig, arrived in ye Bay about 2 oClk in the Afternoon, of ye 18th January and at 4 oClock, The Governor, attended by several Officers, went in two armed Boats towards a part of the Shore where, 6 of the Natives, were, and had been sitting the whole time the Supply was entering the Bay, looking and pointing at Her with great Earnestness; When the Boats had approached pretty near this Spot, two of the Natives got up, and came close to the Waters-Edge, making Motions, pointing to another part of the Shore and talking very fast & loud, seemingly, as if the Part to which they pointed, was better landing for the Boats, they could not however, discern any thing unfriendly, or threatening in the Signs and Motions which the Natives made.--Accordingly the Boats coasted along the Shore in a Direction for the Place, to which, they had been directed, the Natives following on the Beach. In the mean Time, the Governor, or somebody in his Boat, made Signs that they wanted Water, this they signified by putting a Hat over the Side of the Boat and seeming to take up some of the salt Water put it to his Mouth, the Natives, immediately, understood this Sign and with great Willingness to Oblige, pointed to the Westward, and walked that Way, apparently with an Intention to show their Visitors the very Spot. The Boats steered towards the Place, and soon discovered the Run of fresh Water, opposite to which, they landed, and tasting it found it to be very good. The Natives had stopped about 30 Yards from ye Place where the Boat landed, to whom, the Gentlemen made signs of thanks for their friendly Information, at the same time offering Presents, and doing every thing they could think of, to make them lay aside their Fears and advance towards them, but this point was gained only, by the Methods that I have mentioned: and when they did venture to come and take the things out of the Governor's & the other Gentlemen's Hands, it was with evident Signs of Fear, the Gentlemen now having distributed all their Presents among them, returned on Board.

Thus, was our first Intercourse obtained, with these Children of Nature.--About 12 of the Natives appeared the next Morning, on the Shore opposite to the Supply, they had a Dog with them, (something of the Fox Species); The Governor and the same Gentlemen that were of his Party Yesterday went on Shore, and very soon came to a Parley with them, there were some of their Acquaintances among the Number, and these advanced first (leaving their Spears with their Companions who remained behind at a little Distance) as they had done Yesterday); They all of them in a short time became Confident, Familiar & vastly funny took any thing that was offered them, holding out their Hands and making Signs for many things that they saw, laughed when we laughed, jumped extravagantly, and grunted by way of Music, & Repeated many Words & Phrases after Us. The Gentlemen having passed about an hour with them, returned on Board, but could not induce any of the Natives to accompany them there. A Party of Us made an Excursion up an Arm in the North part of the Bay, where we had not been long landed before we discovered among the Bushes a Tribe of the Natives, who at first did not discover such an inoffensive & friendly Disposition, as those I have spoke of, above; for these rude, unsociable Fellows, immediately threw a Lance, which fell very near one of the Sailors, and stuck several Inches in the Ground, we returned the Compliment by firing a Musket over their Heads, on which I thought they would have (Unclear:)broken their Necks with running away from Us. about an hour after, we, in our Ramble, fell in with them again, they stood still, but seemed ready for another Start. One of Us, now laid down the Musket and advanced towards them singly, holding out some Bawbles, and making Signs of Peace; In a little time they began to gain Confidence, and two of them approached to meet the Gentlemen who held out the Presents, the Introduction being amicably settled, they all joined Us, and took the Trinkets we offered them; The same Emotions of Pleasure, Astonishment, Curiosity & Timidity, appeared in these poor Creatures, as had been observed in our first Acquaintances--There were some Old and young Women in this Tribe, whom the Men seemed very jealous & careful of, keeping them at Distance behind some young Men, who were armed with Spears, Clubs & Shields, apparently as a Guard to them. We could see these curious Evites peeping through the Bushes at Us, and we made signs to the Men, who were still with Us, that We wished to give some Trinkets to the Women, on which, One of their Husbands, or Relations (as we supposed) hollowed to them in an authoritative Tone, and one of these Wood-Nymphs (as naked as Eve before she knew Shame) obeyed (Unclear:)or obliged and came up to Us; when; we presented her with a Bracelet of blue Beads for her obliging Acquiescence; She was extremely shy & timid, suffering Us, very reluctantly, even to touch Her; Indeed, it must be merely from the Curiosity, to see how they would behave, on an Attempt to be familiar with them, that one

4

George B. Worgan

would be induced to touch one of Them, for they are Ugly to Disgust, in their Countenances and stink of Fish-Oil & Smoke, most sweetly.--I must not omit mentioning a very singular Curiosity among the Men here, arising from a Doubt of what Sex we are, for from our not having, like themselves long Beards, and not seeing when they open our Shirt-Bosoms (which they do very roughly and without any Ceremony) the usual distinguishing Characteristics of Women, they start Back with Amazement, and give a Hum! with a significant look, implying. What kind of Creatures are these?!--As it was not possible for Us to satisfy their Inquisitiveness in this Particular, by the simple Words. Yes or No. We had Recourse to the Evidence of Ocular Demonstration, which made them laugh, jump & Skip in an extravagant Manner.--In a Tribe of these funny, curious Fellows, One of them, after having had His Curiosity gratified by this mode of Conviction, went into the Wood, and presently came forth again, jumping & laughing with a Bunch of broad Leaves tied before Him, by Way of a Fig-leaf Veil.--Before we took our leave of the Tribe that threw the Lance; they endeavoured to convince Us, that it was not thrown by general Consent, and one of them severely reprimanded the Man who threw it, and several of them struck him, but more to shew Us their Disapprobation of what he had done, than as a Punishment for it.

During our stay at Botany Bay, the Governor. had made himself well acquainted with the Situation of the Land Nature of the Soil &c. &c. which he not finding so Eligible, as he could Wish, for the Purpose of forming a Settlement, He determined, before he fixed on it, to visit an Inlet on the Coast, about 12 Miles to the Northward of this Bay which, our great Circumnavigator, Captns Cook, discovered, and named, (in honour of one of the then Commissioners of the Navy) Port Jackson accordingly, the Governor, attended by a Number of Officers went in 3 Boats, on this Expedition, and the third day, they returned, gave it as their Opinion, that Port Jackson was one of the most spacious and safe Harbours in the known World, and said they had already fixed on a Spot, on which the Settlement was to be formed. In Consequence of this Success, the Idea was entirely given up, of establishing a Colony at Botany Bay, and three days after, the Wind favouring our Designs, the Fleet sailed for Port Jackson and in the Evening of the Day of our Departure, We arrived, and anchored in one of the many beautiful Coves which it Contains, which Cove Sir, the Governor has, (in honour of Lord Sydney), named Sydney Cove.

Though the Description given by the Gentlemen who first, visited this Port was truly luxuriant, and wore the air of Exaggeration, Yet

5

they had by no means done its Beauties and Conveniences Justice, for as an Harbour, None, that has hitherto been described, equals it in Spaciousness and Safety. the Land forms a Number of pleasant Coves in most of which 6 or 7 Ships may lie secured to the Trees on Shore. It contains likewise a Number of small Islands, which are covered with Trees and a variety of Herbage all which appears to be Evergreens. The Whole, (in a Word) exhibits a Variety of Romantic Views, all thrown together into sweet Confusion by the careless hand of Nature. Well, Dear Dick, now I have brought you all the Way to Sydney Cove, I must tell you what we have done, since our arrival in these Seas, & in this Port--what we are doing, what has happened &c. &c.

On the Evening of our Arrival (26th January 1788) The Governor & a Number of the Officers assembled on Shore where, they Displayed the British Flag and each Officer with a Heart, glowing with Loyalty drank his Majesty's Health and Success to the Colony. The next Day, all the Artificers & an 100 of the Convicts were landed, carrying with them the necessary Utensils for clearing the Ground and felling the Trees. By the Evening, they were able to pitch a Number of Tents and some Officers, and private Soldiers slept on shore that Evening. In the Interval of that time and the Date of this Letter, the principal Business has been the clearing of Land, cutting, Grubbing and burning down Trees, sawing up Timber & Plank for Building, making Bricks, hewing Stone, Erecting temporary Store-houses, a Building for an Hospital, another for an Observatory, Enclosing Farms & Gardens, making temporary Huts, and many other Conveniences towards the establishing of a Colony.

A small Settlement has been established on an Island, which is about a Fortnight's sail from this place, and named by Cap.tn Cook Norfolk Island, the Intention of this Settlement I believe, is on account of the fine Pine Trees, of wh the Island is full, and to try what the Soil will produce.

We have discovered an Island in these Seas, never before seen by our Navigators, We have named it, Lord Howe's Island It affords Turtle in the Summer Season, and the Supply Brig, brought away 18 very fine Ones, on which, we feasted most luxuriously, it also, abounds with Birds of the Dove Species, which are so stupid, as to suffer us to take them off the Bushes with our Hands. As this Island is not above 4 or 5 Days sail from Port Jackson, we hope, to have Turtle Feasts frequently: if this be the Case, I suppose We shall have a Ship-load of Aldermen coming out to New South Wales.

As I mean to annex to this Letter, a kind of Journal of each Day's Transaction and Occurrences, I shall pass over many things in this Narrative, and enter immediately on a rough Sketch of the Country of New South Wales, its Inhabitants &c. &c. as far, at least, as We have been able to learn. Botany Bay, Port Jackson, and another Inlet (8 Miles to the Northward of Port Jackson, which Captn: Cook calls Broken Bay,) lie between the Latitudes of 35° & 40° South. This Part of the Coast (which is as much as we have been near enough, to judge of) is moderately high and regular, forming small Ridges, Plains, easy ascents and descents. It is pretty generally clothed with Trees and Herbage Inland; The Shore is rocky and bold, forming many bluff Heads, and overhanging Precipices. On approaching the Land which forms Botany Bay (but I shall speak more particularly to that which forms Port Jackson) It suggests to the Imagination Ideas of luxuriant Vegetation and rural Scenery, consisting of gentle risings & Depressions, beautifully clothed with variety of Verdures of Evergreens, forming dense Thickets, & lofty Trees appearing above these again, and now & then a pleasant chequered Glade opens to your View.-- Here, a romantic rocky, craggy Precipice over which, a little purling stream makes a Cascade There, a soft vivid-green, shady Lawn attracts your Eye: Such are the prepossessing Appearances which the Country that forms Port Jackson presents successively to your View as You sail along it.

Happy were it for the Colony, if these Appearances did not prove so delusive as upon a nearer Examination they are found to do; For though We meet with, in many parts, a fine black Soil, luxuriantly covered with Grass, & the Trees at 30 or 40 Yards distant from each other, so as to resemble Meadow Land, yet these Spots are frequently interrup: in their Extent by either a rocky, or a sandy, or a Swampy Surface crowded with large Trees, and almost impenetrable from Brush-wood which, being the Case, it will necessarily require much Time and Labour to cultivate any considerable Space of Land together. To be sure in our Excursions Inland, which I believe have not exceeded 30 or 40 Miles in any Direction, we have met with a great Extent of Park-like Country, and the Trees of a moderate Size & at a moderate distance from each other, the Soil, apparently, fitted to produce any kind of Grain and clothed with extra-ordinarily luxuriant Grass, but from its Situation, and the Quantity of Wood, though in a moderate Quantity in Comparison with that in other Parts) It is the general Opinion here, that it would be a great Length of Time, and require a vast Number of Cultivators to render it fit to produce Grain enough to supply a small Colony. About 50 Miles to the West, and North West Inland, there appears to be some mountainous Country and from our having seen Smoke on it, now & then, We are led to suppose that it is Inhabited. The Governor intends to visit these Mountains shortly, and I have his permission to accompany Him in this Excursion, but I don't think, he will go, before he has discharged, and dispatched all the Ships for England.

Here is no collective Body of fresh Water, that merits the Name of a River, except, perhaps, after heavy Rains What there is arises from Springs, and forms Swamps and small Rivulets, it is very good in kind, and there is a plenty of it, for two or three of these Rivulets empty themselves into most of the Coves.--In Digging Wells You succeed in some Parts, after having gone 3 or 4 Feet under the Surface, but this water it seems, is only from Drains in others, You shall dig a considerable depth and not meet with any Water. We have discovered a Soil in many Parts of the Country excellently adapted for making Bricks, and a Brick- Ground is already prepared, where 8 or 10 Convicts of the Trade are employed, and they say the Bricks are as good as those made in England. = Here is plenty of Materials for the Mason & Stone-Cutters to practice their art on; and they speak very highly of the Quality of the Stone, as being well-adapted for Buildings. = As a Cement for these Materials, Nature has provided a whitish Marl, which, the Masons think will answer tolerably well; if it should not, they have no resource but in burning Oyster, & Cockle Shells, for no Stone has been yet discovered that will do for Lime.

Of the Vegetable Productions of this Country, and first, of the Trees, We have found three kinds that answer tolerably well for Building, the largest of these is lofty and thick some of Feet in Height before a Branch springs out, and are from in Circumference.--The Leaves and Twigs of this Tree have a warm, aromatic Flavour, and there exudes from the Trunk of them a red astringent Gum: On the Trees being Cut I have seen this Gum gush out like Blood from an Artery. = The next Tree for Magnitude is (they think) a Species of the Mahogany. This does not grow so straight, nor to such a Height or Circumference by far, as the above Tree. = The third kind bears Leaves like a Fir, is remarkably straight and runs up free from a Branch to the Height of Feet, & from 3 to in Circumference, the Wood of it is heavy & hard, and they have discovered that it makes good Shingle, with which they have already covered a large Store-house, and find it to answer very well. It is from this Tree, the Natives strip the Bark for the making of their Canoes, but of the Manner of doing this, By & By.

Cabbage-Trees abound here, it is a beautiful Tree, growing perfectly Straight to the Height of 70, 80 or 90 Feet. The Cabbage is at the Top, enclosed in a Fibrous Network, and about this, large Fan-like leaves spring out.

The Cabbage eats something like a Nut. the Wood of these Trees, (wh. is very soft,) is of great Use to Us, for; cut into proper lengths and split in half, they serve for walling the Huts. = Unfortunately, none of this Timber cuts into good Beams or good Planks, it being for ye most part shattery, and full of Cracks; however, the Carpenters think it may be improved by taking the proper Methods, used for seasoning Timber.--Here is a dwarfish Tree, bearing a long Rush-like Leaf, the Trunk of which yields a Quantity of a yellowish Gum, resembling in Taste, the Storax, the Natives use this Gum as a Glue for sticking the pointed Bone on their Fish-Gigs, it is something singular, that all, of this kind of Trees, and many others appear to have been partly burnt, the Bark of them being like charcoal. Of Fruits Trees we have found a small Fig, and Berries of unknown, species, One bears a Nut, which after some preparation, the Natives Eat, but one of the Convicts has been poisoned by it, in its crude State. As to the Shrubs and Plants and Herbs of this Country "Tis beyond the Power, of Botanists to number up their Tribes.--Among the useful we have discovered, Balm, Parsley, Samphire, Sorrel, & a kind of Spinnage, but, all indifferent in kind a Shrub bearing a Fruit like a Sloe, and here is a Fruit which tastes exactly like the Currant when green, but these Fruits are scarce. The Woods are decorated with a Variety of prettily coloured Flowers, but there is not above 2 or 3 kinds that have any Fragrance I have seen a kind of Myrtle in some few Spots.

The Spots of Ground that we have cultivated for Gardens, have brought forth most of the Seeds that we put in soon after our Arrival here, and besides the common culinary Plants, Indigo, Coffee, Ginger, Castor Nut Oranges, Lemons, & Limes, Firs & Oaks, have vegitated from Seed, but whether from any unfriendly, deleterious Quality of the Soil or the Season, nothing seems to flourish vigorously long, but they shoot up suddenly after being put in the Ground, look green & luxuriant for a little Time, blossom early, fructify slowly & weakly, and ripen before they come to their proper Size. Indeed, many of the Plants wither long ere they arrive at these Periods of Growth,--but then this Circumstance must be considered, they were sown, the very worst Season.

I have, also, enclosed a spot of Ground for a Garden and make the Cultivation of it one of my Amusements. I put Peas, and broad Beans in, soon after I arrived, (February) the Peas podded in 3 Months, the Beans are still (June) in Blossom. and neither of the Plants are above a Foot high, and out of five Rows of the Peas each 3 Feet in length, I shall not get above 20 Pods, however my Soil is rather too sandy, and in some Spots I see Vegetation has a stronger Appearance. If there are any Plants that flourish better than others, it is thought, that these are Yam, Pompkin;--and ye Turnips are very sweet, but small. I opened one of my Potatoe Beds, & found 6 or 7 at each Root; Indian Corn, and English Wheat, I think promise very fair; But on the whole, it is evident, that from some Cause or other, tho' most of ye Seeds vegetate, the Plants degenerate in their Growth exceedingly.

The Plants which we brought here, from the Rio de Janeiro and the Cape of Good Hope look tolerably promising, for ye most part, but some of these have perished, and others appear to be withering.--From the short time we have been here, 'twill be unfair to speak positively on the Climate or the Soil, a Round of y Seasons will decide this Issue.

Having now given You some Account of what these Wildernesses are formed, I'll say a Word or two of their Inhabitants, and first of the Human Species, of which, (though we haved obtained many Intercourses with them) We have been able to learn but little.--They are of a moderate Height, few reaching up to 6 Feet, rather slight than Robust their Complexion is of a reddish, Blackish Soot Colour, filthy & dirty to Disgust; Men Women and Children go entirely naked, scorning a Veil as big as a Fig-leaf, I cannot say their Features are very irregular such as they are, their Lips are rather thick, their Teeth sound, but yellow, dark dingy Eyes, broad, short Noses with wide Trumpet Nostrils which are plugged up with dry drippings, their Hair is black and softish, and has more of a Touselled than a curling appearance That on their Head has the appearance of a full-bottom'd black scratch Wig put on with the Hind part before.--The Men walk very upright, the Women stoop forward a little, are very active & strong, there is something singular in their Manner of sitting and standing, when they have a Mind to stand in an easy Posture it is by resting on one Leg, and fixing the Foot of the other flat on the Inside of the Knee of the Leg on which they are standing, throwing their right Arm obliquely behind them, and taking hold of it with their left hand put across their Back. When they sit, they rest upon their Posteriors and their heels, the Knees sticking up to their Chin; This Position with the Women, when sitting in their Canoes makes a convenient Cradle for the Child, which they lay across their Lap while they are fishing with a Line. In activas they are active The Generallity of them, Men & Women, have Scars in different parts of their Body, which in some, seem to have been cut in par-particular Lines by way of ornament.--Many of the Women, Old & Young, Married & Unmarried have had the two first joints of the little Finger of the left Hand cut off, this Custom being apparently, practised indiscriminately, We do not know what to conjecture of it.--Almost all the Men have had one of the Fore-teeth extracted, but from being so universal we are equally at a Loss as to ye Motive of this Custom, they will sometimes thrust their Fingers into your Mouth to see if you have parted with this Tooth. the Governor happens to want this Tooth, at which they appear somewhat pleased & surprised. We have seen but few with a Bone thrust through the bottom of the Division of the Nose, they likewise want to know if we have the hole in that part, a Fellow picked up a Quill one Day, and was trying whether he could poke it through my Nose, and two or three other Gentlemen's, who were with Me, then shewing Us that he could not wear it in his own, & shaking his Head.--Animals Teeth & Bones stuck in the Hair with Gum is another of their elegant Ornaments. When we have taken hold of these Decorations to admire them, several good-natured Fellows have immediately pulled them off, and presented them to Us.

Among two or three Tribes, with which we have had a Parley, there have appeared 18 or 20 stout young Fellows, seemingly chosen out by way of a Guard to the Women, who always are observed to be at a distance behind them, these Men are besmeared with Red and white Clay, and in such Lines and Circles as to resemble ye Belts, Sashes, & Ornaments of our Soldiers, they are armed with Spears, Clubs, Wooden Scimitars, & Shields, & these peculiarities give them the Appearance of Warriors.

Captn. Hunter, in one of his Excursions up the Harbour met with a Tribe of ye Natives, among whom, were a Number of these Warlike Heroes, and while One or two of ye Elderly Civilians advanced towards Him, These, stood at a Distance drawn up in somewhat a regular Disposition, each having a green Bough in his Hand (an Emblem of Peace among these People). Captain Hunter had invited them to come and take some Bawbles which he held out, but he refused to give them to the old Men who had come up to Him, making Signs, that he wished to give them to the Women, (whom, he saw a small distance behind the Warriors). the old Fellows finding he would not give the Presents to them, hollowed to the Women in a stern Voice, on which, a young, attended by an old Woman (after being called to 3 or 4 times) came forth, but showed evident signs & Emotions of Shyness & Timidity in advancing to take the Presents from Cap.n Hunter's hand. They suffered, (but not without trembling exceedingly,) the Beads to be tied about their Necks & Wrists, this being done, they retired back behind the Guard. Notwithstanding this apparent Shyness & Timidity when in your Reach, Yet, the young Baggages, when at a Distance from Us, make all the wanton significant signs imaginable.--It does not appear that these poor Creatures have any fixed Habitation, sometimes sleeping in a Cavern of a Rock, which they make as warm as an Oven by lighting a Fire in the middle of it, they will take up their abode here, for one Night perhaps, then in another the next Night, at other times (and we believe mostly in ye Summer) they take up their Lodgings for a Day or two in a miserable Wigwam, which they make of the Bark of a Tree, (in ye form annexed), these are dispersed about the Woods near the Water, 2. 3. 4 together some Oyster, Cockle & Muscle Shells lie about the Entrance of them, but not in any Quantity to Indicate, that they make these Huts their constant Habitations. We met with some that seemed entirely deserted, or left for any other Tribe, that might want another Lodging, indeed, it seems pretty evident, that their Habitations, whether Caverns, or Wigwams, are common to all, and alternately inhabited by different Tribes. In the few that we saw, while they had Lodgers the whole stock of Furniture consisted of a Bundle of Spears, 3 or 4 fishing Lines, Shields & Baskets made of ye Bark of a Tree.

They associate (we have reason to think) in Family Tribes, the Eldest assuming a Direction & Government over the Rest, each Tribe, according the number, have 6, 8, or 10 Canoes, in these contemptible Skiffs (which display very little art or Ingenuity) they paddle, (with two things like Pudding stirrers) from one Cove to another even up and down the Coast, keeping as close to the Rocks as possible. The Women make much more Use of them than the Men do, for they get into them only when they want to cross from one Cove to the other, which having reached, they land, leaving the Women in them to fish with a Hook and Line, while they walk along the Rocks close to the Water, and strike the Fish with their Spears, and at this, they are very dexterous, seldom missing their Aim, which indeed is not to be wondered at, for Fish, being their chief Subsistence and their Hooks & Lines not being very plenty, They are obliged to practice this art of taking them daily; When they have caught enough for a Meal, and feel hungry, The Men, call the Women on shore, and haul up the Canoes for them, They then gather up a few dry Sticks, light a Fire under a shelving Rock, (if there is one near,) or a Wigwam, here they sit down and broil their Fish, when it is just warm through, they take off the Skin & Scales, then eat the Fish, Entrails, Bones and all, if not very large.--We have observed, that they chew a Fern Root at the time they are eating the Fish, but this, they spit out, having chewed it with 6 or 8 Morsells of Fish. they eat some kind of Fruit like a Fig, too.--We have given Birds to them which having bearly plucked, and warmed through they devour refusing no part of it. One or Two of them have ventured to taste our Salt Beef & Pork, which they liked so well, that they made signs for more,--The principal Articles on which the Subsistence of these poor Creatures depend, consist of Fish, Water and Fire; (Unclear:)

Their Canoes, Spears, Lines & Hooks are necessary for procuring the first Article--Their Weapons, of Defence consist of a Spear about 14 Foot long and terminating in a sharp point of Bone or hard Wood (whereas their fishing Spear has four Prongs tipped with Bone) they have a hooked Stick for throwing the Spear; a heavy Club, a piece of hard Wood in the Form of Scimitar, and a Shield made of a broad bit of the Bark of a Tree, seem to make up the whole of their warlike Instruments.--Their Canoes are made of the Bark of the Tree, which I have said, somewhat resembles the Fir in its Growth. The manner of taking the Bark off for this Purpose is nearly as follows. After having made a circular Incision through the Bark, beginning 3 or 4 Feet from the Bottom of the Tree, they, by the help of Notches, climb up as high as they mean the Length of the Canoe shall be, where, they cut ye Bark through as at the Bottom, after this is done, they divide it in a straight Line from the top Incision to the bottom, and they contrive that this longitudinal Division of y Bark shall run through the middle of the Notches, which they had cut to climb up by, so that they prove no detriment to the Bark for the Purpose that it is intended. It being cut through to the Body of the Tree, they thrust in sticks between it & the Bark, by way of Wedges. to separate it from the Tree, they then leave them in this Manner 'till the Bark will strip off without using any Violence that might split it. having got it off, they pucker up the Ends and tie them with a tough stringy kind of Bark; & in order to stretch it open we suppose that they place sticks across, and keep them there till the Bark takes the form of a Canoe.--The Article in which, I think they discover the greatest Ingenuity is their Hooks & Lines, the Hooks are of a pearly shell, ground to this shape, (Unclear), the Lines are of a fine Bark nicely shredded & twisted very close and neatly: I have seen some of the Men with Net-Bags, made of this line.--There is one of their Arts which we have not, as yet, been able to come at the Knowledge of. I mean that, of producing Fire so quickly as they seem to do, a Stone appears to be one thing necessary for this Purpose, but we cannot find out what else they use.

As to the Article of Dress I have hinted before they strictly follow the primitive Simplicity of the Adamites and the Evites and it may be said of these rude children of Nature, as of them, "they are naked and not ashamed", and I may add, they are nasty and dirty and not ashamed.

They are wonderfully expert at the art of Mimickry, both in their Actions and in repeating many of our Phrases, they will say--"Good Bye" after us, very distinctly, The Sailors teach them to swear. They laugh when they see us laugh, and they appear to be of a peaceable Disposition, and have a Generosity about them, in offering You a share of their Food.--If you meet with any of them, they will readily offer You Fish, Fire, & Water, they seem to be easily offended, and quick and fatal in revenging an Injury.

In a Word, to sum up the Qualities Personal & Mental, (those at least we have been able to discern) They appear to be an Active, Volatile, Unoffending, Happy, Merry, Funny, Laughing Good-natured, Nasty Dirty, Race of human Creatures as ever lived in a State of Savageness.

They seemingly enjoy uninterrupted Health, and live to a great Age. We have seen One or Two deformed in their Backs & Legs. a poor Fellow showed us a crooked arm w.h he made signs that he broke by falling from a Rock.--

We have reason to suppose, they burn their dead, and throw the Ashes into a Heap; for we have met with 2 or 3 of these Heaps resembling in shape our Graves, One of which we examined and found Pieces of the Human Bone that were not quite consumed.

Only two of Them have ventured to visit our Settlement to whom the Governor gave many presents, and did every that he thought might Induce them to stay, or to come again and brig their Companions; The Objects which must have been entirely new to them did not excite their Curiosity or Astonishment so much as one might have expected. They just looked at them, with a kind of vague Indifference. Of all the Things that have been given them the Axes (Fishing hooks & Lines, or any spare Instrument or Food seem to please them most. The Drum was beat before them, which terrified them exceedingly, they liked the Fife, which pleased them for 2 or 3 Minutes. Indeed Music of any kind does not attract their attention, long together, they will sometimes jump to it, and make a grunting Noise by way of keeping Time to the Tune. I have now given You most of the Particulars relating to the Customs and Manners of this rude Race of Creatures, that we have been able as yet to learn, which must necessarily be very little from their Language being such an inarticulate, unintelligible Jargon.

The other kinds of Inhabitants of these Wildernesses, and first of the Species of Quadrupeds that We have either shot, taken or seen are Dogs, Kanguroos, Opossums, the Pole Cat, Rat & Mouse Species.

The Natives have frequently Dogs with them, and the Governor has procured one of them. In Colour and Shape it resembles the Fox Dog, but the Tail is not so bushy, it has become very tame and domestic. The Natives set one of these Dogs at a Man, whom the Governor employs to shoot Birds and other Animals, and as He found himself in Danger of being Bit, He shot Him dead on the spot, the Natives were extremely terrified at this, and took to their Heels with the greatest Precipitation.--The Animals which Captain Cook describes in his Voyage to New South Wales under the Name of Kanguroo are very numerous here: They feed in Herds of 12. 20 and even 50 together, the Animal does not run, but jumps along on his hind legs, We have shot a great many of them the largest that we have killed, weighed 139 Pounds; ye Tail 17 Inches round. the Flesh, when the Animal is young eats something like Veal, as some think, but for my own part I am puzzled to know what it eats like.--

The Opossum, Pole Cat, & Rat Species are in great plenty, many of each sort have been caught & shot, they are very destructive to our Eggs & Poultry, they have snapped the Head off, two or three of our Hens & Chickens, and then sucked their Blood.--Three or four kinds of flying Squirrels have been shot. Some of the Convicts reported that they saw a Tyger one Evening, but we believe it was one pictured by their own creative Imaginations, You know, to a timorous Man a Bush in the Dark might be easily mistaken for a Tyger.

Birds are of various kinds here: the first, for Size and Food is the Emew, this Bird answers the Description given of it by naturalists very well, 3. 4. 6 of these Birds have been seen in the Woods feeding together, but they are extremely shy, and run with incredible Swiftness.-- Our Grey-hounds got sight of One but could not come near to Him in running, however, the Governors Game-procurer by great chance got a Shot at one of them with a Ball and killed Him. It resembles the Ostrich in most particulars; The Flesh of it eats like young Beef, and one of its Side Bones was more than enough for four of our Dinners. Quails, Pidgeons, Doves Plover, Cockatoos, Beautiful Parrots, Loriquets, Crows, Hawks, and a variety of other kinds of Land Birds have been shot by our shooting Parties. Many of these Birds are beautiful in their Plumage, but There are none that sing half so sweet as our Chaffinch.

Of Water Fowls Ducks, Teal, Heron, Cranes, have been shot, and one Black Swan has likewise been shot, many of these last Birds have been seen, but they are extremely shy, as indeed may be said of all the animals here, which has led us to think that they are harrassed by the Natives. Our Gentlemen sometimes go out for a whole Day, and are not able to get a shot at a single Bird.--

I was one Day on a shooting Excursion and fell in with a Tribe of the Natives, while I was with them, a Crow settled in a Tree that was within shot, on levelling my Gun at it, one of the Natives run up to Me in a hurry clapped his Hand over ye Muzzle of the Piece and cried out several times, Baû Baû Baû Baû! meaning as I conjectured, that I was not to kill it (for they have seen the Effects of the Gun) I complied with his Request, and laughed off the Offence I had seemingly given, at which, he laughed likewise and seemed mightily pleased.--All the Animals, and the Birds that I mentioned above, (where Beef, Mutton, & Veal are entirely out of the Question) make no despicable Meat.--Of Reptiles here are Snakes, Scorpions, Centipedes, Lizards and Guanas, The Insects which prove troublesome, are Musquitos, Sand Flies, Red and Black Ants: Here are Spiders of various kinds, Butterflies, and several sorts of Beetles, and some few Bees have been seen. The Harbours on this Coast are well stocked with a variety of Fish. And we have never set down to Dinner without a Dish of one kind or other upon ye Table since our Arrival here, very often, the Boat is so successful as to catch enough for the whole Ship's Crew, and two or three times we have been able to supply the Officers Tables on Shore. but since the approach of the Winter, the Fish have become scarce, perhaps they go to the Northward as the cool Weather comes on, and return to the Southward with the Summer. The different kinds are, John Doreys, Turbots Soals, but these are as rare as Dolphins in the River Thames, One or two of each, however, have been taken. Mullet, Bream, Snappers, Jew Fish, Sting Rays, Mackerel are very common.-- Oysters, Cockles & Muscles are to be got for a little Trouble. one very small Lobster has been caught, and wonderful to tell, it was red.-- Enormously large Sharks are very numerous in the Harbours, and are very destructive to the other Fish, as well as they are to our Lines & Hooks. We have taken a great many of them, and have found in the Female between 30 & 40 young ones.

George B. Worgan

A Word or Two of the Climate, then I have no more to say of the Country.--It was in January that we arrived here which in this part of the Globe is Midsummer, the Weather has been, for the greatest Part of the time, serene, moderate & pleasant, & warm tho' at times the Vicissitudes from Serenity to Squalls of Wind, Rain, accompanied with terrible Thunder & Lightning are sudden, and violent and from a dry sultry Heat, to a chilly Dampness (occasioned by heavy Night Dews) considerable. The Thermometer on Shore in the Shade has been up to 85 & 90 at Noon and by Sunset has fallen to 50 or 60, the Fall of 25 or 30 Degrees is common.

The Thunder and Lightning are astonishingly awful here, and by the heavy Gloom that hangs over the Woods at the Time these Elements are in Commotion, and from the Nature of the Violence done to many of the Trees, We have reason to apprehend that much Mischief may be done by Lightning here. Indeed we have experienced its fatal Effects since we have been here, for one Night 6 Sheep 1 Lamb, & 2 Pigs that were lying under a Tree, were all killed and the Tree violently riven. Two or three other Trees near ye Settlement have been riven in the same Manner by Lightning since we came here. The prevailing Winds here are S.W & S.E., Sea and Land Breezes are pretty regular, in fine Weather. On the whole, it may be said, we have more of what may be called agreeably warm, Dry, Clear, Serene Weather than Sultry, Rainy, Foggy, or Boisterous. It is just (June 18.th) now the middle of Winter, and the Weather is for ye most part clear, pleasant & moderately warm, but it is very (Therm cold 44 at times) in the Mornings & Evenings. and I think we have more frequently a rainy, damp, chilly Day than we used to have a Month ago but no Snow, nor Frosts, and We have, and shall have all through the Winter green Trees in abundance to look at, that is more than you can say in your Winter Master Dick.

Now I'll tell you what we have done with the Convicts, how they are disposed of, employed, &c. &c.--The Governor had on the Passage made himself acquainted with the Trade and Occupations of each: Accordingly, when they were landed, the Men that could be spared from the principal Business of clearing the Ground were set at their respective Employments, as occasion required such as the Carpenters, Sawyers, Shingle makers, Stone Cutters, Masons, Brick Makers Black-Smiths, &c. these were divided into Parties, and one of the most promising among the Party, was made an Overseer to the Rest.--

The Provost Martial, Constable, and Patroll, (Offices appointed by the Governor) were instructed to keep them within certain Limits;

17

Notwithstanding these Precautions to keep them at their Tasks, they found means to evade this Vigilance, and straggle into the Woods, they even had the Impudence to go over to Botany Bay, (wh. is only 8 or 10 Miles by Land from this Port) and offer their Services as Seamen On Board the French Ships, (by the by, It strikes Me that I have never mentioned the Circumstances of these Ships arriving at Botany Bay, I will look back and if I have omitted it in this Narrative, I will tag it to the Journal which I mean to annex to this) The Officers would have nothing at all to say to them, and drove them away.--Ten or 14 of Them would take their Provisions (which is served them once a Week) and instead of going to Work skulk about the Woods, and return by the Time of serving Provisions again. These with many other Misdemeanours committed on their Voyage and since their arrival here, convinced the Governor that if he tried them any longer with a lenient Government, He would be making the Just suffer for the Unjust. Therefore the Day, on which His Commission, and the Laws by which the Colony was to be governed were read: He told them, that he was sorry to find, He could no longer govern them by Lenity.

For this Reason, he was determined for the future, every Trespass however trivial, every Violation of the Laws or Orders should be severely punished. Thefts, He assured them, would never more be pardoned, but if detected, they should have every justice done them in their Trial, and if found Guilty, the Laws should take their Course: To the Industrious He promised every Encouragement, but those that would not Work and were found Idling in the Woods, their Provisions should be stopped, and they should have corporal Punishment.--It is to be feared, that among such a Number of Delinquents, there are some innately bad and incorrigible, who are deterred from pursuing their vicious Inclinations only from the Fear of Punishment; and who will still be villanous, when they can be so secretly For, notwithstanding all that the Governor said to them, there are daily complaints of petty Larcenies, and other Offences:--Two desperate Villains have been detected in stealing, tried in the Criminal Court[1], found guilty, condemned, and in order to strike a terror into the Rest, led a few hours

---

[1] Four Courts can be held here, a Civil, Criminal, Martial and Admiralty they are composed of the Naval and Military Officers, the Judge Advocate of the Settlement presides at the Civil & Criminal. If 5 out of 7 concur in Opinion, Sentence of Death may be put in Execution. The Governor can Commute, Mitigate or Pardon a Sentence.

after from the Court House to the Place of Execution and hung up, nevertheless, they still are hardened and persist in their Crimes, some, by way of Punishment, have been put on a Rocky Island & kept there a Week or Two on short Commons, and there is no End to Flogging Them--The greater part of The Women Convicts are a shocking abandoned set. The Governor took every Precaution to prevent an indiscriminate Intercourse with Them & the Men, and as he thought Marriage among them might effect the good Purpose he meant,

They had his Permission to Marry, and 20 or 30 of Them are already married, but the Misfortune is, one half of them have asked the Governor if the Chaplain cannot Unmarry, in short, they are a vile pack of Baggages continually violating all Laws, and disobedient to all Orders. The Disease, that Scourge of Mankind has made its appearance among them.

* * * * *

Journal (January 20--July 11 1788)

I think I hear You Exclaiming as you cast your Eyes up to this new starting Place--"What the D--ce not done Gossiping yet!" No dear Dick I have not near done yet; Prithee my dear good Brother, do but consider the Distance that separates Us, which, is nearly that, of Antipodes. for when we are getting up in the Morning, You have hardly entered into your first Sleep; when it is the Depth of Winter with Us, you are enjoying Richmond Hill So that considering our Situation, with Regard to You, Were I to write as much as would fill up 100 Reams of Paper and every Word to sett off for your Country as soon as it dropped from my Pen, and to Scour & Scamper away Helter-Skelter through Southern and Northern Latitudes, by the Time that the last set off to which, I should give the Office of whipper-In, The First Word will not have reached one quarter over the Seas that divides Us, at the time the last is tumbling out of my Mouth; Moreover, I expect an Advantage in relating these Matters in a Multiplicity of Words for I shall let fly each with such an impulsive Velocity against its leader, that by the time the last gives its Impulse, the whole will have received such an irresistable Velocity, as to make their Way against the Resistance of Rocks, Seas and contrary Winds and arrive at your Street-Door with a D (Unclear:)--1 of a Suscitation; Therefore rally your Patience Brother Dick--and take your Seat on one side of the Fire, and while I fancy Myself seated on the other, I will relate You a string of little Transactions, Occurrences, Excursions & Adventures which I could not introduce in the preceding Narrative without thrusting them in Head and Shoulders to the utter Confusion of the whole: and as these Incidents have happened in almost an unknown Part of the World, I am unwilling to omit them, because I think they may, possibly, afford You and Your Friends half an hours Amusement, and a new Topic to Reflect and Comment upon in your social Meetings--I shall relate them just as they stand in my rough Journal, In a Word, I mean this, as a minute Detail of the Circumstances, which have influenced the Opinions which I have given You in the former, respecting the Country, its Inhabitants &c. &c. I shall perhaps stumble upon Repetitions, but I will vary as much as possible the Relation of them, but you must excuse Me stopping to attend to Points, Syllables, The's, And's, and all such tagging materials, These I will beg You to put in for Me, before You lend it your Friends, whom, with You, I sincerely hope the World goes cheerly.

Oh, now I think of it, You are a Musician so
Volti Subito.

* * * * *

January 1788

Sundy 20th.

Between 7 and 8 oClock this Morning the Sirius accompanied by the Lady Penrhyn, Charlotte, Prince of Wales, Borrowdale, Fishbourn, and Golden Grove Transports anchored in Botany Bay. We found here the Supply Tender, the Alexander, Scarborough and Friendship, Transport, which left us at Sea on 25th of November 1787 to proceed with the utmost Dispatch, but the Supply Tender (on Board of which, was Governor Phillip) had arrived no more than 2 Days, and the 3 Transports only one Day before Us.--Captn. Hunter of the Sirius, waited on the Governor, immediately, and about 10 oClock they together with several other Officers landed on the South Shore, there were 8 or 10 of the Natives standing at a little Distance from the Beach, but, on the Boats landing they ran away into ye Woods

However, the Governor obtained a Parley with them before He returned on Board.--a Boat was sent to haul the Seine which had been very successful, having caught as much of Mullet, Bream, Sting-Rays, and other kinds of Fish as served the Sirius's Crew.

Mond.y 21st

Governor Phillip, Captn. Hunter & several other Officers set out early this Morning, in 3 Boats, to visit a Harbour about 12 Miles to the Northward of this Bay, discovered, and named by our great Circumnavigator, Captn. Cook, Port Jackson.--In the mean while, the Governor, had ordered, that some of the Artificers and a Number of Men from the Sirius should be sent to the South Shore to clear the Ground, and Dig Saw Pits.--Some of the Natives came down to Day both on the South & North Sides of the Bay, and behaved very funny & friendly, they expressed a little Anger at seeing us cut down the Trees, but it was only by jabbering very fast & loud, they did not like the Soldiers, and made signs for us to take them away, before they would venture to come near Us. One of them was bold enough to go up to a Soldier and feel his Gun, and felt the point of the Bayonet, looked very serious, & gave a significant Hum!

The other Businesses of the Day, were the exploring different Arms of the Bay, hauling the Seine.

Tues. 22dn

The Artificers and Sirius's Men were employed as Yesterday, felling Trees, clearing the Ground, Examining the Bay &c.

The Natives came down, in the Morning and the Afternoon, & were very friendly, jumping & jabbering in a strange Manner.

There was a laughable Circumstance to day, A pot was boiling in which there was some Fish for the Workmen's Dinners, One of the Natives (who never had seen or felt hot Water before) very deliberately put his Hand in to take a Fish out, when, feeling a very smart Sensation, he gave an amazing Jump squalling out most Hideously, on which, his Companions seeing us laugh, joined Us very heartily, while the poor Fellow was skipping about & blowing his Fingers. In the Evening, we happened to make

* * * * *

Finding that I had missed this side of Paper, I shall (however irregular it may come in here) Insert the Account of the two French Ships which did Us the Honour of a Visit, during our short stay at Botany Bay, they expected to find a great Progress made, towards the Establishment of the Colony, and even hoped, that we should be able to afford them some Refreshments of the vegetable kind. We had seen two large Ships in the Offing (and a Ship in these Seas is almost as rare a thing as a Man of War above Westminster Bridge) three Days before we left the Bay, but the Wind blowing right out, they could not get in, till it favoured them somewhat, on the Morning that it favour'd our sailing for Port Jackson.--The Names of the Ships & Commander &c. &c. I have mentioned on the other side of this leaf.

The Compliments being received & returned, we took our leave of them and ply'd out of the Bay, where, they were now moored.

The Officers were rather reserved in making us acquainted with the Route they had taken, and the Discoveries they had made since they arrived in these Seas, but gave Us to understand, that they had been very far to the Northward, that Captn. Cook was extremely correct in the Narrative of his Voyages, and that He had left them very little to discover or Describe in this part of the Ocean.

They told Us they had been very unfortunate in their losses of Boats, Officers, & Seamen.--On the North West Coast of America they lost two large Boats, in which were 22 of their People, & all drowned. the third Part of the Number were Officers: Again, at the Navigator's Islands, the Natives to the Number of a 1000 as they judged, attack'd them, when they were on shore watering, and with one

Volley of Stones, suddenly discharged at the same Instant; destroyed two of their Boats, killed 14 People, and desperately wounded several others; One Captain & 5 Subalterns were among the Number killed, those that were unhurt, or only wounded, fired a Volley of Musketry on the Natives as they were retreating, and saw, as they think, about 30 fall this was all the Revenge they took--We could not learn on which side the Provocation began, but the French Officers, feared that their Seamen had given some Offence, as they had been here for some time and had lived on the most friendly Terms with the Natives.--These Ships remained at Botany Bay about 5 Weeks, during which Time No People could show more Attention, Respect &, Civility, than their Officers did to Us, and We were equally zealous in showing the like Dispositions towards them. In a Word, there was a constant Succession of mutual good Offices passing between Us; We visited each other frequently, sometimes the Parties going by Water, at other Times by Land (for it is only 8 or 10 Miles over) and the little Difficulties and Fatigues which ye Voyagers or the Travellers underwent, were thought amply compensated, if they could attain a social Intercourse with one another,--Govr. Phillip had expressed his Wishes to Mr. Perouse to be of any Service to Him in his Power, & Mr. Perouse made use of this Offer by sending some Dispatches to be forwarded to Europe, by our Transports.--They hoped to be in Europe themselves in 18 Months.

* * * * *

A very successful haul of Fish in the Seine, which the Natives seeing, they all, threw up their Arms, and set up a shout of Astonishment, looking (as we thought) at the Sun We gave them plenty of Fish, which gratified them exceedingly.

Wed. 23d

Our Transactions were much the same as Yesterday. About 5 oClock in the Afternoon, the Governor and his Party returned from the Expedition to Port Jackson, of which they spoke very favourably, as being an excellent Harbour, and the Land about, far better adapted for the forming of the Settlement on. Accordingly the Masters of the Transports received Orders to prepare their Ships for sailing the next Morning.

Th. 24th.

The Wind not favouring our Departure this Morning, the Boats were employed in getting on Board Grass & Water for the Cattle. At Day-light, to our great Astonishment, We observed two large Ships in the Offing, which seemed to be plying to get into this Bay, by Noon, We could, by the help of our Glasses, discern that they had French Colours flying; but the Wind blowing strong, right out of the Bay, they could not possibly get in, and it coming on Misty rainy Weather, we lost Sight of them.

Fri. 25th

Could see nothing of the French Ships this Morning, the Governor sailed for Port- Jackson, in the Supply Tender, but the Wind coming on to blow hard, right into the Bay, the Sirius and Transports could not possibly get out.

Sat 26th

About 8 oClock this Morning, we, again, discovered the two strange Ships, which now were standing in for the Bay, with a fine leading Breeze. On their Arrival, an Officer was sent from the Sirius on board the Commodore's Ship, which was distinguished by a white Flag at the Main-Top-Mast Head;--On the Officer's Return, the Commodore's Captain waited on Captn Hunter to pay his Respects. It seems they are the two Ships, which the Court of France sent out on Discoveries in August 1785. The one called the Astrolabe, the other the Boussoule under the Command of Monsr. Perouse

About 10 oClock the Wind favouring our Departure, the Fleet got under Sail, (leaving the two french Ships in the Bay) by 8 oClock the same Evening, we were all safe at anchor in Port Jackson.

They Supply arrived here the Evening before, & Captn. Hunter waited on the Governor who was on shore, where, he had caused the English Flag to be displayed. At Sun-set the Governor, the principal Officers of the Settlement, and many of the private Soldiers, drank His Majesty's Health & Success to the new Colony.

Sun 27th

Early this Morning a Number of the Artificers and Convicts were sent on shore with the necessary Implements for clearing the Ground felling Trees, in Order that the Tents might be pitched for the Battalion

The Governor marked out the Lines for the Encampment, and to prevent the Convicts straggling into the Woods, he appointed a Provost Martial, a Constable and a party of ye Soldiers to take all Men up, that were found out of the Boundaries. The Boats that were sent to haul the Seine were very successful, they met with some of the Natives, who behaved very friendly, even helped them to haul the Seine on shore, for which kind Office they were liberally rewarded with a Portion of the Fish. The Governor gave strict Orders, that the Natives should not be offended, or molested on any Account, and advised that wherever, they were met with, they were to be treated with every mark of Friendship, In case of their stealing any thing, mild means were to be used to recover it, but upon no account to fire at them with Ball or Shot.

Mon 28

The Employment to Day has been much the same as Yesterday, and most of the Tents are pitched. Some few Officers slept on shore.

Captn Hunter, Lt. Bradley, & the Master of the Sirius set out to explore and take a Plan of the Harbour.

T. 29th

The Governor, having fixed on a convenient Spot for the Cattle they, were all landed to Day. The Frame of the Governors House was landed, and the Carpenters employed in putting it up.

February

Tu:5th

In the Course of the last Week all the Tents of the Battallion, the Labaratory, and Hospital, and several of the Civil Officers Tents have been pitched,--likewise those for ye Men and Women Convicts, the Governors House got up, a Spot of Ground enclosed, and some culinary Seeds put in. The Plants that we brought from Rio de Janeiro, and the Cape of Good Hope all landed and put in the Ground a few Beans, Peas, small sallad, that were sown on our arrival here, have come up and appear at present very luxuriant: On the First Day of this Month, We had a vast deal of heavy Rain. Thunder & Lightning, and the next morning 5 Sheep, 1 Lamb. & 2 Pigs, were found dead, lying under a Tree, which was riven in a violent Manner by the Lightning: A small Store House is begun, for the Reception of some of the Provisions--All the Convicts Men and Women, are landed: Many of the Men, and one Woman are missing.

Sat 9th

Last Thursday the Governor's Commission, and the Commission for establishg the Laws by which the Colony is to be governed, were read by the Judge-Advocate of the Settlement. There was some little Ceremony observed on this Business. Orders had been issued (the preceding Day) that every Body, on Shore, and from on Board the Ships that could be spared should attend. Early in the Morning the English Ensigns were displayed on Board the Ships & on the Shores, about 9 oClock the Battalion were drawn up on the Spot of Ground that had been cleared for a Parade, about 10, the Governor, all the Officers of the several Departments, the Convicts, Men & Women were assembled within a Square formed by the Military Arrangement; The Judge-Advocate of the Settlement then proceeding to the Business of reading the several Commissions, which, being performed, the Battalion fired 3 Volleys of Small-arms, the Band playing the first part of God save the King, between each Volley. The Governor then addressed the Convicts in an excellently adapted Speech, accompanied with many judicious Exhortions As well as I can remember it was to the following Purport--He began by Observing that they had now heard the Laws read, by which they were to be governed, and they might depend upon it, that they should have their full Force: For He was sorry to find, that there were many among Them not be governed by Lenity, as he had frequently tried this mode of Government, by having already, repeatedly forgiven them Crimes, which they had committed in the Passage out, and since their Arrival here, and they had as constantly abused his Lenity, by similar Trangressions, all which he said, He would freely forgive and forget, but for the Future, he assured them, the Law should take its Course.--He was convinced, he told them, that there were a Number of good Men among them, who, unfortunately, from falling into bad Company, from the Influence of bad Women, and in the rash Moment of Intoxication, had been led to violate the Laws of their Country, by committing Crimes which in the serious Moments of Reflection, they thought of with Horrour & Shame, and of which now, they sincerely repented, and would be glad by a future Conduct to retrieve their Characters; but sorry was he to add, that he feared there were some Men & Women among them, so thoroughly abandoned in their Wickedness, as to have lost every good Principle: Therefore, from henceforth, he declared, that however it might distress his Feelings, every Crime, from the smallest to the greatest Magnitude should meet its Punishment, which the Law inflicted. He observed likewise that many of them, since they had been disembarked, instead of assisting in the necessary Work of forming the Settlement, were found skulking in the Woods, and came to the Camp only at the appointed times for the serving of their Provisions to them, for the Future, all such Idlers, as were found beyond the Limits, the Provost Martial, and the Patrol received Orders to take up and Imprison, & that in Case of their running from the Patrol, they would be fired at with Ball: Moreover, He assured them, that those who would not Work, should not Eat, for, the good Men, he promised, should not be Slaves for the Bad, their daily Labour should be much easier, on account of the Warmth of the Climate than the Common Labourer's in England, but That, they should perform, or Starve,--He gave very good Advice & Encouragement to the Women, telling them, as well as the Men, & promised that good Behaviour should never go unrewarded by Him.

They had his Permission to Marry, and proper times would be allowed for the making up their little Agreements amongst each other, but after a certain hour in the Evening, any Man seen in the Woman's Camp, the Sentry would have orders to fire at with Ball, & in all indiscrinate Intercourse with the Women, the Offenders should be severely punished.

February 1788 Sat 9th.

He concluded by assuring them that it was in their own Power by a steady Perseverance in a Series of good Conducts to make the Day of their Transportation to this Place, the happiest Day they had ever seen; but once more, he would give them his Word, that for the Future, no Crimes whatever should go unpunished, observing, that not to punish the Bad, was doing an Injustice to the Good, therefore, Henceforth, The Laws should take their Course.--

In this Address, I thought the Governor, spoke with a Feeling and a Concern, that does Honour to his Humanity, and it is really a Pity, he has the Government of a set of Reprobates who will not suffer him to indulge himself in a Lenity, which he sincerely wishes to govern them by.--The Convicts were allowed the Rest of the Day to themselves, and the Governor, entertained, as many of the Officers as he conveniently could, at Dinner.

Sat. 9th.

A Party set out yesterday for Botany Bay, by Land, to pay a Visit to the French Officers, from whom, they met with a very polite and cordial Reception. They informed our Gentlemen that a Number of the Convicts had been over, and applied earnestly to be taken on Board; One of Them promised to pay a Sum of Money for his Passage, on his Arrival in Europe Others, offered their Services as Seamen, and required no other Reward than their Provisions for the time of Serving, but the Officers of these Ships so far from Countenancing them, threatened, that if they were seen to skulk about there, they would send them Back to Us.--

Our Gentlemen met with a good deal of swampy, Rocky Ground in their Journey and on the whole it was tedious, but the Civilities and hearty, friendly Treatment, which they received from the French Officers very amply recompensed all their Fatigues.

The same Day, Captn Clonard (the French Commodore's Captain) came round by Water, in a Boat from Botany Bay, to wait upon Govr. Phillip. He brought with Him, from the Commodore, some Dispatches for Europe which the Governor, had politely made an Offer to forward by the first of the Transports that he should Dispatch from this Place for England.--A Kanguroo was shot to Day, the first that has been procured since our arrival in the Country--8 or 10 Natives passed not far from the Ship this Morning, in 5 Canoes, when they got near the Rocks, many of the Men got out, and by the help of a Spy-Glass, I could see them very busy in striking the Fish with their Spears, and I saw them take two or three tolerably large ones in this manner; the Women, remained in the Canoes employed in fishing with a Hook & Line, the Fish, they caught, appeared but small, after having caught a good many, they went on shore a little way up in the Wood, lit a Fire, and sat down round about it, in the Afternoon, they got into their Canoes, and returned, passing by the Ship again, they houllowed, jabbered & pointed.

1788 Feby Sat 16th

In Consequence of the Governor giving his Permission for the Convicts to marry, We had no less than 14 Marriages last Sunday,-- and Notwithstanding, the Admonitions which the Governor gave them on the Day the Laws were read, We have had no less than 6 or 7 Trials for petty Larcenies, some were sentenced to be Flogged, and some to be put upon a barren Island, in the Harbour, there to remain for a Week, to live on Bread and Water; These Thefts are generally, of Provisions, and a very aggravating Circumstance in them is, that the Foragers are allowed as much of Salt Beef, Pork, Peas, Flower, Rice, Bread & as good in Quality, as any Officer on the Settlement, but still they cannot be contented.--On Thursday last, the Supply Tender sailed for Norfolk Island, on Board of Her was a Detachment from the Settlement, consisting of Lt King (2dn. of ye Sirius), Mr. Cunningham, Master's Mate, & Wm. Jameison my first Assistant, 2 private Marines, 12 Men and 6 Women, Convicts, 6 Months Provisions, Implements of Husbandry, Artificers Tools, Seeds, Sheep, Goats & Fowls. for the Purpose of trying what that Island may produce.

Wed. 27th.

Nothing material has occurred since the 16th. till to Day, when, three Convicts, were tried in the Criminal Court for stealing Provisions, they were Convicted upon the clearest Evidence and sentenced to be hung; Accordingly, about 6 oClock the same Evening, they were brought to the fatal Tree, the Battalion under Arms, Provost Marshal, & the Peace Officers attending, at the Execution, when, John Barrett, the most notorious of the Criminals, was tied up, and hung the usual time;

28th

The other two, were respited till 6oClock the next Evening, when, being brought to the place of Execution, the Governor was pleased to send down a Commutation of their Sentence upon the following Conditions. The One was to execute the Office of Hangman, as long as He remained in the Country, the other to suffer Banishment on some adjacent Island. I need not tell you they readily agreed to these Conditions.--Some one who should in future perform the disagreeable Task of Hangman, was an Officer which, considering what a class of Men the major Part of our Colony consisted, would probably be much wanted; for the Man who had agreed to execute this Office, failed so much in his Duty, (either from Timidity or Feeling) in the Execution of Barrett, that, our Sheriff. was under the disagreeable Necessity of mounting the Ladder Himself, in order to fix the Halter, so here was an Opportunity of establishing a Jack Ketch, who, should in all future Executions either Hang or Be Hanged

We have made some Discoveries this last Week, One is that the Tree, which I have said grows something like the Fir, answers very well for the making of Shingle, Our other Acquisition is the lighting on a Soil, which is seemingly fitted for making Bricks, and 8 or 10 Convicts of the Trade are now employed in the Business.

March

Sundy. 2dn

The Governor, Lt. Bradley, Master of the Sirius accompanied by some other Officers set out this Morning, in 3 Boats to look into, and to explore a Bay, which is about 8 or 10 Miles to the Northward of Port Jackson discovered and named by Capt. Cook Broken Bay.

Mony. 3d

--A Bird has been shot to Day. which answers the Description given by Dr. Goldsmith, of the Emew, it resembles the Ostrich its Flesh proved very good Eating, & Four of Us dined off, from one of the Side-Bones

Sund. 9th

The Governor, and his Party returned this Afternoon from Broken Bay, it seems that it affords good Shelter for Ships, that the Entrance is bold, Plenty of Fish to be had, but for Spaciousness & Convenience it is not to be compared with Port Jackson.--

They met with a vast number of the Natives here, some of wh they thought they had seen before, at Botany Bay, indeed, it is pretty clear, that they wander up & down the Coast, going to the Northward in the Winter, and returning to ye Southward (as we expect to find) in the Summer. The Natives, were very friendly to them, offered them Fire & Water, were extremely full of their Fun, laughing, Mimicking & Frisking about. The Behaviour of one of the Women was rather singular, she took a great liking to the Governor's Great Coat, and as she could not influence Him to give it to her, by soft persuasions in her own language, She tried Jumping, Capering, and various Wanton Anticks would do, but these not succeeding according to her Wishes, She began to Weep, in a most lamentable strain, put on languishing Looks, in short practised all the Siren's Arts, but the Governor considering that this importuning Lady had done very well, seemingly, without a great Coat, and that it was a Comfort to him in his present Expedition, which it would be endangering his health to part with, He was obliged to persist in the Refusal of what, this Damsel had so whimsically and pathetically supplicated.--In one part of the Bay, on their Landing rather late in the Evening, when, it was raining & blowing, an elderly

Man came up to them, presented a lighted Stick, and invited them to a Cavern of a Rock, which was in Sight, and where he had a cheerful Fire, but as the Governor was for taking another Route, They could not comply with this Gentlemans Invitation, at which He seemed not a little displeased; However, This Man, visited them next Morning, and stay'd with them two or three Days, and by his Attention had prepossessed the Governor in his Favor, till, on the third Day, when, this trusty Friend, having taken a wonderful longing for a Spade, which he saw one of the Boats Crew using, took an Opportunity of making off with it, but, being seen, was stopped, and brought to the Governor, who, made signs for Him to go about his Business, giving him at the same time, a smart stroke with his open Hand, on which, the Gentleman was very very angry & Run & called his Comrades, but a Musket being fired over their Heads, they all scampered away into the Woods like Rabbits into a Burrow, however, the next Morning, they came down where the Governor had Tented all Night, & were Friends again.

Another curious Circumstance happened to them, while they were on the Business of exploring this Bay; They had landed, where there was a great many of the Natives; and in one of their Huts, the Governor, saw a large Crawfish, which, He Bartered for, giving the Owners of the Fish a Hatchet, and distributing Bawbles among many of Them whom, he thought might have a share of it, The Governor, now took the Fish, and was walking down towards the Boat with it, when, one of the Natives meeting Him, snatched it out of his Hand, and ran up with it to the Hut, where he had bought it, The Governor took no Notice then, but got into the Boat; soon after, they saw the same Fellow running down to the Boats hollowing and holding out the Fish, his Comrades, having told him, as they imagined that they had given something for it, however, the Governor, & the Gentlemen went on shore again, would not accept of the Fish but went up to the Huts where he got it, and took back all the Presents he had given them, this Conduct, was a great matter of Surprise & Mortification to them.

Sund.y 16

Four Convicts that were sent out a little Distance from the Settlement to cut Rushes came in to Day, and acquainted the Governor that 10 of the Natives had attacked them, who, after throwing a few Spears and Stones at them, retreated; One of the Convicts shewed a small Wound in his Breast, which, he had received from a Spear a P

Wed 19th

The Supply Tender arrived to Day from Norfolk Island. They told us, it was with great Difficulty & Hazard, they Landed the Provision and Stores for the little Colony. The Shore being extremely rocky; and the Surf beating very high. which, they have Reason to think from the Situation and Form of the Island is mostly the Case. In their Passage to this Island, they fell in with an Isle in the Latitude of and Longitude which had never been before discovered Lt. Ball, named it (in Honour of Lord Howe,) Lord Howe's Island, on Landing they found a great many Turtle, 18 or 20 of which, they brought away with them, they likewise, met with several Birds of the Dovekind, which they come so near to, as to knock down with a short Stick;. Nothing very remarkable of vegetable kind was found, Trees of the Palm kind were numerous. The chief Acquisition that we hope may accrue to our Settlement. from the falling in with this Island, is the Turtle off which, we hope to have many a Feast. Dick.

Tues. 25.--

To Day, the Lady Penrhyn, Charlotte, & Scarborough, being cleared of the Stores for the Settlement were discharged from Government Service, and will sail for China, as soon as they can fit for Sea. The East India Company having, before they left England, engaged them to go their for a Cargo of Tea; & as the Captains think of arriving in England in 14 or 15 Months, I shall put Letters on Board the Three Ships, for You, Denton, and all my Friends

We have had some Trials this Month in the Criminal Court but none of the Delinquents have been capitally convicted.--

The principal Business going on a shore, is the Building an Hospital, Store houses, Huts for the Officers; Enclosing Ground for Gardens. Many of the Officers have had 2 Acres of Land allotted to each, but 'tis not given to them as their Right & Property, because the becoming so, depends upon Government. at least, this is what I hear,--All the culinary Plants that have come up, degenerate exceedingly, Peas, Beans, Cabbage Plants &c do not thrive, & many of them have withered. Yams, Potatoes (Unclear:)Pumpkins, Turnips, Indian Corn look somewhat promising. The Governor has appropriated an Island, in the Harbour, to the Use of the Sirius, on which we have Landed our live Stock, enclosed a part of it for a Garden, and a put a good many different Seeds in.

The Live Stock of the Settlement, in general Increase and Multiply,

April

Sund: 13th

The Governor, & Captain Hunter accompanied by some other Officers, went on an Excursion down the Harbour, and made a Discovery of an Inlet which led into an extensive Space of Water forming a fine spacious Harbour, they likewise fell in with some Water which they had Reason to suppose was a Lake.

Mond. 21st.

Cap.tn Hunter & Lt. Bradley & the Master of the Sirius set out this Morning to take a Survey of the new Part of the Harbour, which was discovered on the 13th Inst.--The Governor, accompanied by some of the Military Officers, the Surgeon of the Settlement, and a Party of Marines set out this Morning to penetrate Inland some Miles to the Westward, Had you seen them, they would have put you in Mind of a Gang of Travelling Gipsies, for each of them had a Snapsack on his Back, with 8 Days Provision, some had Kettles, & Iron-Pots; In order that they might find their Way back again, they Notched all the Trees that stood in the Direction of their Route. On the 28th Instant they returned, having penetrated about 30 or 40 Miles Inland, they walked over a vast Extent of fine Meadow Ground, where, the Trees were at a greater Distance from each other, than they are in the Country round about the Settlement, The Soil, they found was far superior in Quality; They saw some very high mountainous Land, which, at some other Opportunity the Governor means to Visit, and I hope to have his Permission to accompany Him in that Excursion.

31st--

We have had a few Trials, & plenty of Flogging, but I believe the Devil's in them, and can't be flogged out.

May

5th

The Lady Penrhyn Transport, and Supply sailed to Day the Former for China, the latter for Lord Howes Island to endeavour to procure us another Turtle-Feast,--In the Course of this last Week, We have had another Execution of a very young Lad but an old hardened Offended, who, on his arrival at the fatal Tree, said, that he was now going to suffer a Death, which he had long deserved.

Mon 12th

The Charlotte and Scarborough Transports, sailed, to Day for China, and as it is a matter of Doubt, whether those Ships will not arrive in England, before any of the Transports, Can, that sail direct for England, as soon as they can be cleared of their Stores. I have put 2 or 3 Letters on Board them for You & all my Friends, indeed, it is natural for Us, in such a distant part of the World, to snatch greedily at every Opportunity to convey our Hopes & Wishes to our Friends.

Tus. 13

I walked out to Day, as far as the Brick Grounds, it is a pleasant Road through the Wood about a Mile or Two from the Village, for from the Number of Little Huts & Cots that appear now, just above Ground, it has a villatick appearance. I see they have made between 20 & 30,000 Bricks, and they were employed in digging out a Kiln for the Burning of them. I afterwards walked to the publick Farm, where, I find they have turned up 8 or 10 Acres of Land, and they talk of putting some Corn in the Ground soon. The Sheep die very fast from some Cause, The Cows & Bulls thrive I think, as do the Horses. The Hogs don't thrive. The Poultry do not increase very fast.

Wed. 14th

I have had a most delightful Excursion to Day with Captn Hunter and Lt. Bradley, We went in a Boat about 12 Miles up the Harbour. For 3 or 4 Miles the Harbour forms a narrow arm, which at high Water, has the appearance of a River, the sides of this Arm are formed by gentle Slopes, which are green to the Water's Edge. The Trees are small and grow almost in regular Rows, so that, together with the

Evenness of the Land for a considerable Extent, it resembles a Beautiful Park. We landed quite up at the Head of this Branch where a fresh Water River runs into it, but which, at this time was dry in many places. We walked about two Miles up the Country in the Direction of this River; the Ground ran in easy ascents and Descents, the Soil was extremely rich, and produced luxuriant Grass.

We now and then, in our Walk, met with Clusters of a very delicate looking Tree, the Trunks of some of Them were 12. 14. 20 Inches round, covered with a green Bark, the leaves of a peculiarly beautiful Verdure and growing like the Fern, but more delicate. Having extended our Excursion as far as we wished, we returned to the Place where we landed and after regaling Ourselves with a cold Kanguroo Pie and a Plum Pudding, a Bottle of Wine &c, all which Comforts we brought from the Ship with Us, We returned on Board.

Frid 16.th

The Foundation Stone of the Governor's House was laid to Day, An Inscription engraved on Copper, to the following Purport is to be placed among the Foundation Stones, viz. The date of the Governor's arrival in this Cove, and the Date of the laying of the Foundation Stone of His House.

Mond 19--

They have begun to unlade the Transports, and land the Stores, and it has this Day been publickly announced that some of the Transports will sail for England in 6 Weeks, so a scribbling we will go. I shall put a Letter on Board each Ship for You. Pray don't neglect to forward those that I intend to Inclose in yours. & Pray Mr. Dick have You had an Opportunity yet of Sending Me a Packet of News? who is the King? the Queen? the Ministers? whats the Whim? our whim will soon be, to go Naked, for You know, "When we are at Rome &c". As for my part I shall be obliged soon to make a Virtue of Necessity for I have torn almost all my Cloaths to pieces by going into the Woods; and tho' we do not want for Taylors, We do, Woolen Drapers. Our Excursions, put me in Mind of your going a Steeple Hunting, We sometimes, put a Bit of Salt Beef, or Pork, Bisket, a Bottle of O be joyful, in a Snapsack throw it over our Backs, take a Hatchet, a Brace of Pistols, and a Musket, and away we go, scouring the Woods, sometimes East, West, N. S. if Night overtakes us, we light up a rousing Fire, Cut Boughs & make up a Wig-Wam, open our Wallets, and eat as hearty of our Fare as You, of your Dainties, then lie down on a Bed, which tho' not of Roses, yet we sleep as sound as You do, on down; I enjoy these little Rambles, and I think you would, however, I think it is hardly worth your while to come and try them.

Fr: 21st

A poor Convict who is on Recovery from a long Sickness, having rambled a little way into the Woods, to pick some wild Balm for Tea returned this Evening, having been wounded in his Back by the Natives with a Lance, part of which was sticking in the Wound, when the Surgeon came to Him,, He said that another Convict was with Him, whom, they wounded and beat very much, and then, carried him away. The Man said, they had given no Offence that he knew of, and that the Lance was thrown suddenly at them.

24th

I accompanied Captn Hunter & Lt. Bradley to Day, upon an Excursion to the Point of Land, that forms the South Head of the Opening of Port Jackson, They went for the Purpose of ascertaining the Latitude of it, which from the Result of many Observations proved to be. We met nothing very remarkable. We saw two Natives at a Distance in the Woods, but they would not be sociable. We likewise saw under us, for we were standing upon a tremendous Precipice from which you looked down into the Sea, (but not without being Giddy) 5 or 6 Canoes, in which were 8 or 10 of the Damsels of this Country, jabbering and Fishing. We hollowed to them, and They, to us, I tied my Hankerchief to a piece of Wood, and threw it down into the Water, which, presently one of them paddled after, & taking it up between her Thumb, and Finger as if it was----and after turning it round two or three times gave it a Toss, with the utmost Indifference, into the dirtiest Corner of the Canoe, chattering something at the same time If that is the Way You treat my Favours Madam, says I Ill keep my Hankerchiefs to----There is something singular in the Conduct of these Evites, for if ever they deign to come near You, to take a Present, they appear as coy, shy, and timorous, as a Maid on her Wedding Night, (at least as I have been told Maids are) but when they are, as they think out of your Reach, they hollow and chatter to You, Frisk, Flirt, and play a hundred wanton Pranks, equally as significant as the Solicitations of a Covent-Garden Strumpet. I cannot say all the Ladies are so shy and timorous on your approaching them, for some shew no signs of Fear, but will laugh and Frisk about You like a Spaniel, and put on the Airs of a Tantalizing Coquet. indeed, if it were not for the nauseous, greasy, grimy appearance of these naked Damsels, one might be said Sat 24.th to be in a state of Tantalism, whenever they vouchsafe to permit Us to come near them; but what with stinking Fish-Oil, with which they seem to besmear their Bodies, & this mixed with the Soot which is collected on their Skins from continually setting over the Fires, and then in addition to these sweet Odours, the constant Appearance of the excrementitious Matters of the Nose which is collected on the upper pouting Lip, in rich Clusters of dry Bubbles, and is kept up by fresh Drippings; I say, from all these personal Graces & Embellishments, every Inclination for an Affair of Gallantry, as well as every Idea of fond endearing Intercourse, which the Nakedness of these Damsels might excite one to, is banished. And I can assure You, there is in some of them a Proportion, a Softness, a roundness, and Plumpness in their Limbs & Bodies, were they but cleanly, that would excite tender & amorous Sensations, even in the frigid Breast of a Philosopher.

Would "stop a Druid in his pious Course Nor could Philosophy resist their Force."

Sund. 25--

The Supply Tender, arrived in this Cove to Day, from Lord Howe's Island, but O! Woeful News, for our Alderman-like Stomachs. Not a single Turtle! so, from having had for this ten day's past, liquorish Chops from the Idea of 4 or 5 Turtle- Feasts on her arrival, we are now all Chop-fallen; The consolatory Reason that our Turtle-Connoissures assign for this Disappointment, is, that from the Winter Season being too far advanced, the Turtle do not go on Shore.--A Soldier brought in a Shirt, a Jacket, and a Hat to Day which, he said he found near to the Place where the poor sickly Convict was wounded, on Friday last, and, as the Jacket & Hat were known to the very Man's, who was with the Convict wounded, We have reason to apprehend that the Natives killed him, and took him away somewhere.

Mond 26th

A Trial came on to Day in the Criminal Court of a Seaman and Marine belonging to the Sirius, for beating & wounding in a most cruel Manner another Man, a Seaman of the same Ship. I, being the Surgeon of the Sirius, and the first of the Faculty who saw the Man, whom they had so cruelly treated, was obliged to attend the Trial, to give my

Opinion, how far his Life was endangered from his Wounds; They had nothing to Say in their Defence, therefore, they were sentenced to receive 500 Lashes each.

Wed 28th

I had an Inclination to Ramble to Day, therefore, as Captn Hunter and Lieutt. Bradley were going to the Point of Land which forms the North Head of the Entrance of Port Jackson, in order to ascertain its Latitude, I took my Gun, and accompanied them, We had to Row 4 or 5 Miles down the Harbour before we landed, We then, had to ascend a steep Rocky, Hill, thickly covered with Brush- Wood, after walking about 2 Miles, we gained the Summit of the Head Land, from which We had a very extensive View, several Leagues out at Sea; Now, (says one of Us) if we could but see a Ship from England steering for Port Jackson, Aye, replies I, then I should get a Letter from my Brother Dick, and perhaps a good Cheese. Ay Ay says Captn Hunter, there would be general Rejoicings in Port Jackson if we could carry them the News of a Ship from England coming in. While the Gentlemen were Astronomizing, to get the Latitude, I & my Man Friday were rambling about, to shoot a few Birds.

By 12 oClock they had taken the necessary Observations, and returning, we made a Circuit over to a part of the Hill, where we observed a great Fire, we found it to be the burning of a Heathy brush- Wood, which we supposed the Natives had set on Fire for some Purpose, but what, we could not Conjecture, We observed likewise, Fires of this Nature, in several other Parts, of the Country, the Wind was blowing very fresh to Day and perhaps this might favour their Designs, if they had any at all, in burning this Stuff; indeed, we have remarked, that, whenever the Wind blows strong, there are a Number of these kinds of Fires about the Country, I have been induced to impute them to accident, from the Natives carrying lighted touch-wood about the Country with them; By the Bye, does not this Circumstance of their being so careful of preserving Fire as long as they can seem to imply, that the producing of it is a Work of great Labour to them? for they even carry the lighted Sticks in the Bottom of their Canoes.

Well, to go on with our Ramble, We got down to the Water-side again, where we left the Boat, and just as we were thinking of setting down for our cold Repast, Mr. Bradley discovered one of the Natives in a Cavern of a Rock, he was lying close down, and there was a little Girl about 4 or 5 years old beside him, they seemed to have been watching Us very anxiously. We went up to the old Adamite, who seemed to be past sixty. He did not discover much Fear, but the poor little Girl was exceedingly frightened at Us and cried and crouched behind the old Man whenever we looked at it.

We shot some Birds and gave them to the old Gentleman, which, after he had barely plucked, he put on his little Fire, and when about warm through, He eat very greedily, Bones, Entrails and all. We let him see the fatal Effects of the Gun, by showing him a Bird in a Tree and then shooting it, on seeing the Bird fall dead, he looked at the Gun with Astonishment, and seemed as afraid of it, as a Woman is, who thinks it may go off, loaded or unloaded. We have been always cautious in letting the Natives see that it is necessary to put anything in the Gun to do Execution with it, and it is a Weapon that keeps them in great Awe, Many of them will not come near You till you have laid it down, which they will make signs for You to do.

Frid 30th

A most Shocking Spectacle was brought to the Hospital this Evening: Two poor Creatures, Convicts, had been sent a few Miles up the Harbour, to cut Rushes, for thatching the Huts, and this Afternoon a Boat was sent to bring them down again, when, they found them lying among some Bushes, and murdered in a most horrid Manner by the Natives, Three Points of Spears were taken out of one Man, two of which had Transfixed Him in the Back the Points sticking some Inches out of his Breast a large Piece of his Skull, including the Eye seemed to have been cut out with an Axe. In the other Man, no wound was discovered from Spears, but he appeared to have been struck with some heavy broad Weapon over his Face, as that Part was black and bloody--The Natives had not stripped them of their Cloaths, nor had they taken their Tents away, but none of their Tools could be found. The Governor, means to take a Party of Marines to morrow Morning, and go to the Place where this Murder was committed, to endeavour to find out the Cause of these Hostilities: For it is his Opinion, with many others, that the Natives are not the Aggressors.

Sat. 31st

This Morning the Governor attended by 3 Marine Officers, the Surgeon of the Settlement, and 10 or 12 Private Marines all armed set out for the Spot where the above Murder was committed.

This Afternoon, it was rumoured, that some of the Convicts had murdered two of the Natives, and 3 Convicts were taken on Suspicion, but as no clear Evidence could be produced to prove the Fact, they were acquitted; However there appeared some Probability of the Truth of the Report, and that the Murder of the two abovementioned Convicts was an act of Revenge, taken by the Natives on some Account, for they were Murdered the afternoon of the Day, on which it was said the 2 Natives were killed, it was asked in the Course of the Enquiry, what was done with the Corpse of the Natives, when, it was supposed that their Companions towed them off.

June

Sund: 1.st

This Evening, the Governor, & his Party returned; They met with, between Two and Three Hundred of the Natives, all, armed, with several Bundles of Lances, Bludgeons, Wooden Scimitars, Stone-Hatchets & Shields.--The Governor & the Rest went up within 50 Yards of them, & halted, the Governor then, having given his Dagger to one of the Gentlemen, and appearing quite unarmed, advanced singly, on Which, one of the Natives, gave his Spear & Club to one of his Companions and met the Governor, soon after the Parley became general, the Rest of the Gentlemen, and many of the Natives having joined, they could not see any of the Tools which, they had taken from the Rush-Cutters, among them, neither could they make out by any Signs the Discovery of the Cause of the Murder, the whole Intercourse with them was begun, and ended amicably. However, Their having thus assembled in this formidable Manner, it seems probable, that they had some Expectation, of our revenging the Death of the Convicts, and were equally prepared to be hostile, as disposed to be friendly, according to our Behaviour toward them--

Mon. 2dn

About a Week ago, a fine She Goat belonging to one of Gentlemen, was found Dead, and some of the Fleshy Parts cut off, and to Day two Men were taken up on Suspicion of having killed this Goat, and made a Pie of some part of it, but it appeared that they found the Goat dead, its Entrails torn out and otherwise mangled as if some Animal had been eating of it, and as it was at this time perfectly sweet, and one of the Men was to be married the next Day, they took the Liberty of cutting some of the Meat off, to make a Pie for the Wedding-Dinner.

Wed. 4th

This being the Anniversary of His Majesty's Birth Day, Governor Phillip had prepared, for the Celebration of it, with every Mark of Loyalty and Distinction, he could think of. At Sun-rise the British Flags were displayed on Board the Ships, and on the Shore. The Sirius, and Supply fired 21 Guns each; This Ceremony they repeated at 1 oClock, and at Sun-set. At 12 oClock the Battalion was drawn up be-

fore the Governor's House, where, they fired three Vollies of Musketry, the First part of God Save the King being played by the Band
between each Volley, after this Ceremony, the Officers of the Battalion, together with the Naval & Civil Departments, proceeded to the
Governor's House, to pay our Respects to the Governor, who received
Us with great Politeness, and congratulated Us, on being the first of
His Majesty's Subjects, who celebrated this Day in New South Wales:
He had previously given a general Invitation to the Officers to dine
with Him; and about 2 oClock We sat down to a very good Entertain-
ment, considering how far we are from Leaden-Hall Market, it
consisted of Mutton. Pork Ducks, Fowls, Fish, Kanguroo, Sallads, Pies
& preserved Fruits, The Potables consisted of Port, Lisbon, Madeira,
Teneriffe and good old English Porter, these went merrily round in
Bumpers. The Toasts after Dinner were, the King, Queen & Royal
Family, the Prince of Wales, Prince William Henry, after this Toast,
the Governor, in a very facetious and judicious Manner, mentioned the
Necessity there was of having a County in order to circumscribe the
Situation of our new Settlement, He would therefore, take this Oppor-
tunity of giving it the Name of Cumberland County, mentioning the
Limits to be Botany Bay to the Southward, Broken Bay to the North-
ward, and some high Land (which he would call Landsdown and
Carmarthen Hills) about 40 or 50 miles to the Westward,--He then
gave as a Toast, The County & the Cumberland Family. In the Course
of the Afternoon the Governor had occasion to step into an adjacent
Room, when; it was intimated by some one to pay Him a flattering
Compliment, and every Gentleman standing up & filling his Glass, we
all with one Voice gave, as the Toast, The Governor and the Settlement, We then gave three Huzza's, as we had done indeed after every
loyal Toast, The Band playing the whole Time.--We had hardly seated
ourselves again before the Governor entered, He said "Gentlemen I
heard You, and I thank You heartily for the Honour you have done
Me, and filling his Glass, drank our Healths, wishing Harmony &
Unanimity throughout the Settlement, promising that nothing should
be wanting on his Side to promote it.--About 5 oClock we broke up,
and walked out to visit the Bonfires, The Fuel of One of Which, a
number of Convicts had been two Days collecting, and to one who had
never seen any bigger than Tower Hill Bonfire on these Occasions, it
was really a noble Sight, it was piled up for several Yards high round a
large Tree; Here, the Convicts assembled, singing and Huzzaing; on
the Governor's Approach, they all drew up on the Opposite Side, and
gave three Huzza's, after this Salutation, A Party of them joined in

singing God Save the King.--The Governor stayed about 20 Minutes, and then, with many of the Officers returned Home, where there was a cold Repast, for any Body disposed to take Supper, about 11 oClock all were retired, and I with Cap.tn Hunter and several other Officers of the Sirius returned on Board.

In Consequence of this being the first Celebration of His Majesty's Birth Day in New South Wales, Governor Phillip, had been studious to distinguish it with every Sentiment of Joy, Zeal and Affection in his Power, accordingly, He had issued his free Pardon, to all the Convicts that were in Confinement for Trial, or under Sentence of Punishment for Crimes committed since they came to the Country. Each Convict was allowed a Pint of Grog, and all Work, was suspended for the Day, Every Private Soldier drank His Majesty's Health &c Health in a Pint of Porter, and every Seaman, in an additional allowance of Grog, and all this, at the Governors own Expense. In a Word every Heart beat with Loyalty & Joy.--

June 5th

Notwithstanding the Governor's Indulgence Yesterday, it was found that while many of the Convicts were rejoicing at the Bonfire, there were others practising their old Custom of Thieving, and many of the Officer's Tents & Huts had been robbed. One Fellow was detected as he was making off, For the Officer happened to be in Bed, and jumping out, seized his Hanger, and knocked the Fellow, down, his Head is cut very much, but it is to be hoped that he will live to be tried & hung. One Officer's Chest was broke open, and robbed of 12 Pair of Stockings & other Articles. Did You ever hear of such a set of Reprobates!

Mon. 9th.

Two of Captain Hunter's Servants having gone on Shore Yesterday Noon, to take a Walk in the Woods, and not being yet returned, we were apprehensive that they had missed their Way, or that some Accident had happened to them, therefore Boats were sent up and down the Harbour close along the Shore with Directions to the Officers of them, to Fire a Musket now & then. I having a Mind for a Ramble, offered, with three other Gentlemen, as a Volunteer to go into the Woods, in search of Them, therefore arming Ourselves, and equipping our Snapsacks, we went on Shore, and directing our Course N.W. Inland We walked till 3 oClock in the Afternoon, hollowing, and firing our Guns every half hour, but not being able to meet with them, we determined upon staying out all Night, accordingly We laid down our Bread an Cheese Wallets, make up a Wig-wam of green Boughs, cut some dry Ferns for a Bed, lit two or three rousing Fires near our Hut, and set down to Dinner. We sung the Evening away, and about 9 oClock retired to Rest, taking it by turns to keep watch, and supply the Fires with Fuel.

About 8 oClock next Morning we set out again to find these poor Pilgrims, who had neither any defensive Weapon, nor Provision with them. We now directed our Course (for we had a Compass with Us) S.S.E. & about 11 oClock, we got down to one of the Coves of the Harbour(Unclear:) not hearing or seeing any thing of Them here, and our Provision nearly out, We walked along the Shore, hollowing, and Firing, till we got abreast of the Ship, We then went on Board, when, we were agreeably informed, that our Fishing Boat, having gone up the Harbour this Morning, they met with them, and took them on Board they were in the very Cove, that we walked down to in the Morning. We did not meet with any thing remarkable in this Excursion. We walked over a vast Extent of rich Land and through some pleasant Valleys, and the Soil seemed fit for producing any kind of Grain, but from its Situation, the Quantity of heavy Timber growing upon it, to render it fit for Cultivation, it would require a vast Number of People, and Teams of Cattle, & a great Length of Time.

23rd

We are just now under great Tribulation about our Bulls and Cows, for they have been missing for some time & there is One of the Convicts who committed a Robbery some time ago, for which if taken, he will certainly be hung, who is supposed to have driven off the Cattle, as they were missed about the same time that he was, Many Parties have been out in different directions, some said they thought they saw the Print of the Cattles Feet, and a Man's near it, however We have Reason to fear they have strayed so far, that they will never be brought back again, if they would but turn wild they might still, perhaps, be of Use to the Country, but we fear that the Natives will kill them, if they fall in with them.

Sun. 29th

No Tidings of our Cows & Bulls yet, but the Man who committed the Robbery, and was supposed to have driven them off is appre-

George B. Worgan

hended, He was taken near the Brick Ground, almost in a starving Condition, He was immediately tried for the Theft, as was also the Man who robbed the Tent on the 4th of June, they both of them pleaded Guilty, and were hung last Wednesday

The Man who was suspected of having driven the Cattle away, declared, he had not seen them. Their Loss, if it proves one, will be rather a Misfortune for our Colony, & as an additional Calamity the Sheep, both of the Public, & Private Stocks, die very fast.

July

2nd

It has this Evening been announced that two of the Transports will sail for England on the 10th. Instant, & two more on the 12th.- I shall put Letters on Board of each, for You, & many of my Friends, so that you will receive One among them all probably just to tell you where I am, and that wherever I am, or may be, I shall hope, Wish & Pray for Your, & Their uninterrupted Health & Happiness. I have written a very long letter, similar to this to my Friend Mr Mein of Fowey, & I am thinking to put His & Yours on Board different Ships, so that if his, or Yours should Miscarry, You or Him can communicate some Accounts of your Infant Colony. Though, if they neither of them arrive, You will still have a chance of hearing of it, as I make no doubt, there will be Narratives Published, & if I can learn, that One Gentleman intends to give it to the Public, I will recommend You & yr Friends to his in preference to any other, because from his Genius I am certain it will be the most Entertaining, Animating, Correct and satisfactory of any that may appear.

July 11th

I am told there will be another Publication by Debrett in Piccadilly, which gives an impartial Account of the Voyage, and a Description of this Country. It will be written by a Captain Tench I believe, belonging to Battalion here. But the other Publication which I referred you too in my Note on the 2dn. Instant will be written by D. Collins Esqr.--the Judge-Advocate of our Settlement--This will just serve to Prepare You & Your Friends for any of the Publications that may come out, it will do, in short for a Fire-side Chit-Chat with your Friends, while the Printers are compiling & Composing the others, but it will by no Means do for a Correct an full Description of the Country, My Situation on Board the Ship will not admit of my collecting all the Incidents Occurrences, Remarks &c and if I had Matter, I have neither Genius nor Abilities to Relate it in a tolerable Manner. I am keeping by me an Account of the Voyage &c. &c. in a Series of Letters which You shall have the Reading of when I return Home, They are something fuller & more accurate than this

George B. Worgan

The Ships sail to Morrow Morning therefore, as I find I have no less than 31 Letters (& 5 of them almost as long as y') to Close, Seal, Enclose & direct, I must Conclude
Believe Me your very affectionate Brother
G B Worgan
P.S. I have sent you 2 Letters beside this in different Ships

THE END

Also from Benediction Books ...
Journal of a Voyage to New South Wales
John White
Benediction Classics, 2011
208 pages
ISBN: 978-1849025188

Available from www.amazon.com, www.amazon.co.uk

The Journal of a Voyage to New South Wales is complete with sixty-five plates of non descript animals, birds, lizards, serpents, curious cones of trees and other natural productions..

The Church That Had Too Much
Anita Mathias
Benediction Books, 2010
52 pages
ISBN: 9781849026567

Available from www.amazon.com, www.amazon.co.uk

The Church That Had Too Much was very well-intentioned. She
wanted to love God, she wanted to love people, but she was both ham-
pered by her muchness and the abundance of her possessions, and
beset by ambition, power struggles and snobbery. Read about the sur-
prising way The Church That Had Too Much began to resolve her
problems in this deceptively simple and enchanting fable.

About the Author

Anita Mathias is the author of *Wandering Between Two Worlds: Essays on Faith and Art*. She has a B.A. and M.A. in English from
Somerville College, Oxford University, and an M.A. in Creative Writing from the Ohio State University, USA. Anita won a National
Endowment of the Arts fellowship in Creative Nonfiction in 1997.
She lives in Oxford, England with her husband, Roy, and her daughters, Zoe and Irene.

Anita's website:
    http://www.anitamathias.com, and
Anita's blog Dreaming Beneath the Spires:
    http://dreamingbeneaththespires.blogspot.com

Wandering Between Two Worlds: Essays on Faith and Art
Anita Mathias
Benediction Books, 2007
152 pages
ISBN: 0955373700

Available from www.amazon.com, www.amazon.co.uk

In these wide-ranging lyrical essays, Anita Mathias writes, in lush, lovely prose, of her naughty Catholic childhood in Jamshedpur, India; her large, eccentric family in Mangalore, a sea-coast town converted by the Portuguese in the sixteenth century; her rebellion and atheism as a teenager in her Himalayan boarding school, run by German missionary nuns, St. Mary's Convent, Nainital; and her abrupt religious conversion after which she entered Mother Teresa's convent in Calcutta as a novice. Later rich, elegant essays explore the dualities of her life as a writer, mother, and Christian in the United States-- Domesticity and Art, Writing and Prayer, and the experience of being "an alien and stranger" as an immigrant in America, sensing the need for roots.

About the Author

Anita Mathias is the author of *Wandering Between Two Worlds: Essays on Faith and Art.* She has a B.A. and M.A. in English from Somerville College, Oxford University, and an M.A. in Creative Writing from the Ohio State University, USA. Anita won a National Endowment of the Arts fellowship in Creative Nonfiction in 1997. She lives in Oxford, England with her husband, Roy, and her daughters, Zoe and Irene.

Anita's website:
http://www.anitamathias.com, and
Anita's blog Dreaming Beneath the Spires:
http://dreamingbeneaththespires.blogspot.com